FORGOTTEN NO MORE

The Korean War Veterans Memorial Story

CAROL M. HIGHSMITH AND TED LANDPHAIR

FEATURING PHOTOGRAPHS BY CAROL M. HIGHSMITH

CHELSEA PUBLISHING, INC., WASHINGTON, D.C.

Col. Thomas T. Jones was among the first Americans awarded the new congressionally authorized Prisoner of War Medal, "for honorable service while a prisoner of war," on July 25, 1988. Note the barbed wire surrounding the American eagle. Jones also received the Bronze Star medal with valor and a Legion of Merit citation.

Forgotten No More:
The Korean War Veterans Memorial Story

Published by Chelsea Publishing, Inc., in association with Cooper•Lecky Architects, WorldTravel Partners, and Event Management Group.

Chelsea Publishing, Inc.
6856 Eastern Avenue, NW
Washington, DC 20012

Design and composition: Robert Wiser, Archetype Press, Inc.

Printing and binding: Monte Nixon, Noble Graphics

ISBN: 0–9620877–3–4

Carol M. Highsmith is a Washington, D.C., architectural photographer whose lens has documented several monumental renovation projects, including the restoration of Pennsylvania Avenue. She and her husband, Ted Landphair, have co-authored five books: *Pennsylvania Avenue: America's Main Street, Union Station: A Decorative History of Washington's Grand Terminal, Embassies of Washington, The Library of Congress: America's Memory,* and a book that took them to every state in the United States, *America Restored,* all featuring Highsmith photographs.

Ted Landphair is a Peabody Award-winning writer and editor. He is a reporter at the Voice of America.

Photography Credits
Carol M. Highsmith: front cover; pages 4–6, and 52–95
National Archives: back cover; pages 2, 12–13, 21, 22 (bottom), and 23–30
U.S. Army Military History Institute: 9–11, 15–18, and 22 (top)

Cover: *Dawn catches the lead troopers.*

Front endleaf: *This rendering, by renowned architectural delineator Paul Stevenson Oles, was the first pictorial image to gain approval of the Fine Arts Commission. Originally drawn in soft pencil on vellum, it demonstrates how the troop statues and etched mural of the Korean War Veterans Memorial work together in a landscape setting. The low curb on the left lists an honor roll of the twenty-two nations that fought together under the United Nations mandate.*

Frontispiece: *In what was dubbed the "foxhole relief operation," a Marine transport helicopter brings in a load of battle-weary marines, while in the foreground, more troops await the signal to load up and replace the men on the line. The Marines routinely "rotated" men between the front lines and rear areas, where a shower, change in clothes, hot grub, and even a movie were sometimes available.*

CONTENTS

TRIBUTE

Many answered the call to duty in an inhospitable place.

The following pages unfold the story of a memorial that has taken ten long years to evolve from dream to reality. As the work progressed, members of the Korean War Veterans Memorial Advisory Board often commented with wry humor that the war was "easy" by contrast; it took only thirty-eight months. Literally hundreds of people have put in endless hours creating this important memorial.

There is one man, however, perhaps more than any other, whose steadfast dedication and leadership helped forge this great tribute to military service. His name was General Richard G. Stilwell. He served as commander of the Fifteenth Infantry Regiment in the Korean War in 1952 and 1953, then returned to the peninsula as a four-star general in command of United Nations forces in Korea from 1973 to 1976. He was chairman of the Korean War Veterans Memorial Advisory Board from its inception in July 1987 until his death on Christmas Day, 1991.

It is hard to imagine a more intelligent, sensitive, articulate, and thoughtful leader. There is no question that he was the spiritual visionary who both challenged and inspired the design team. Every Korean War veteran owes him a debt of thanks—as do all Americans. As this great memorial was created to insure that the veterans of that bloody conflict not be forgotten, we hope its presence will also insure that General Richard G. Stilwell remains in our minds and hearts forever.

W. Kent Cooper, AIA   William P. Lecky, AIA
Cooper•Lecky Architects
Designers of the Korean War Veterans Memorial

INTRODUCTION

It was not called a war. But the "police action" on the Korean Peninsula certainly felt like a war—a filthy, fearsome, though just war—to the men and women who "policed" it. More than fifty-four thousand Americans died in the Korean conflict from 1950 through 1953, or of their injuries later. Half a million South Koreans and other United Nations troops fell, and more than a million GIs and their allies brought home wounds and nightmares and other terrible souvenirs. It was the last foot soldier's war, with a howling, swarming enemy attacking in force, bayonet to bayonet. The last trenches. The final foxholes. The last black-and-white war. Look now at the gritty battlefield photographs and see the GIs' eyes, blackened with grime, sunken from fatigue, glistening with tears. But steeled with resolve.

The years have fogged the memories of that time. We call it "The Forgotten War," and even when it raged it was out of mind in much of a nation weary of war and longing to get back to the good life. It was a far-off dispute, a vexing hot spot in a Cold War, waged with diplomats' words along with infantrymen's guns. Except for the widows and families, this was not the shared national crusade so recently won in The Big One. Antiwar vitriol had not yet found a voice, but neither had collective national gratitude. Yellow ribbons were one war away.

Cpl. Tony Viator of New Iberia, Louisiana, waits for orders for this Twenty-fourth Infantry Division before boarding a C-47 transport plane at Ashiaya Air Force Base for a flight to the Korean front in July 1950. These were among the first U.S. combat units committed, and they fell victim to some of the worst atrocities of the war.

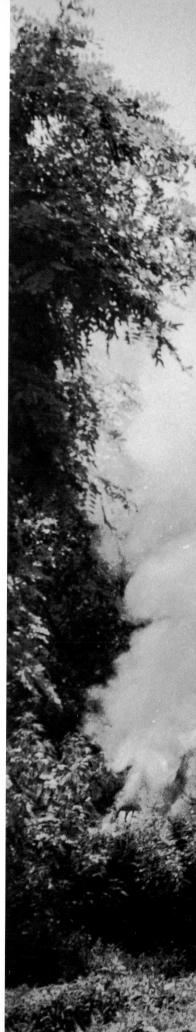

Above. *The 38th Parallel, already well marked as the demarcation between American and Soviet occupation forces in Korea, took on added significance on the date printed on this border sign. It was on June 25, 1950, that Kim Il-sung's forces poured over the border and invaded the South.*

Opposite. *An American tank moves past a burning North Korean vehicle, as a wartime dispatch put it, "somewhere in Korea." UN forces had vast armor superiority, but the peninsula's mountainous terrain often forced commanders to use tanks for stationary artillery support. Problem was, tank shells are designed to pierce armor, not explode inside enemy targets.*

To the nation's schoolchildren, MacArthur and Ridgway and Clark are just old, dead guys, if their names are noted at all. The veterans of Inchon and the Pusan perimeter, of the Punchbowl and Pork Chop Hill and Heartbreak Ridge, and of a hundred other muddy, stinking, frozen places in Korea, are gray or gone. But these gallant patriots who carried freedom's standard there are forgotten no more. The haunting Korean War Veterans Memorial is a nation's belated tribute to their heroic deeds, and to the service of those whose support made heroism possible. Not a bust of one general or a roll-call of the dead, it is a solemn salute to the gunners, mechanics, sailors, cooks, nurses, airmen, and thousands of other men and women in uniform who repulsed communist aggression on a remote peninsula at Japan's door—and, by inspiration, chipped the first crack in communist totalitarianism in Europe and the rest of the world as well. Few words, and no names, encumber this place. Faces—thousands of faces—and nineteen figures in battle gear lead us all out of a sylvan wood into the reality of battle and its terrible sacrifices. But this is not a memorial that glorifies war, or even heroism. It proclaims a broader message about the willingness to serve in a citizens' army that lies at the heart of our nation's democracy.

10

CHAPTER ONE

Such Assistance as May Be Necessary

Overleaf. *The smoke and aerial trails left by the rocket attacks of the U.S. Marine Eleventh Regiment rocket batteries are used by Communists as a guide in returning fire. A Marine helicopter helps solve the problem of counter-artillery fire by flying the launchers and ammunition to a new site, a short distance behind the front lines.*

Viewed through the looking-glass of history two generations after the fighting and dying, the Korean War seems so compact, so manageable. So forgettable. Three short years. One limited thumb of land, with the combat never spilling beyond. There was Machiavellian international intrigue and political posturing all the while for sure, and fears of a nuclear midnight. But all in all, it was a tidy, old-fashioned war to all but the men and women who fought it and those who loved them.

The 38th Parallel of latitude in the Northern Hemisphere is not even a line on most maps, let alone a border, natural boundary, or militarily defensible line. But as World War II wound down to certain Allied victory, the United States government, which had had little contact with remote Korea but was nervous about Soviet expansion into the gut of the Pacific Rim, proposed cutting the old Japanese-held kingdom roughly in half at the 38th Parallel once the peace was won. According to military historian Clay Blair, "a Pentagon Army colonel [had] looked at a school map for 'thirty minutes' and with complete disdain for terrain, or established lines of communication or trade or indigenous political institutions and jurisdictions or property ownership, proposed slicing the Korean peninsula in half at the 38th Parallel." The Soviet Union, America's cunning, Johnny-come-lately Pacific wartime partner, would occupy the northern half, the United States the South, with the intent of disarming the Japanese and paving the way for Korea's long-subjugated people to eventually hold free elections that would unify the country.

"Little Joe," a South Korean orphan adopted by a medical company of the Twenty-fifth Infantry Division, proudly displays a captured North Korean weapon to Cpl. Joseph Bennice of Schenectady, New York. Front-line troops had little time for fleeing civilians, because of the language barrier and because their arrival often portended a Communist attack.

Following V-J Day, Soviet troops entered Korea in August 1945, advanced to the arbitrary demarcation line, and made it imaginary no longer. They promptly cut all railroad and telephone lines and halted the movement of population north to south. U.S. forces were planted in Seoul and elsewhere in South Korea, but the American nation, tired of war and disinterested in a strange land whose people they hardly knew, soon wanted the troops out, wanted them home. A way was found through the fledgling United Nations, which called for countrywide Korean elections. When the bellicose Soviets flatly refused, the UN went ahead with elections in the South. Syngman Rhee, who from exile in Shanghai had long struggled to oust the Japanese from his homeland, was chosen to lead the theoretically united Republic of Korea. But the Soviets ignored the election and set up a puppet Communist dictatorship in the North at Pyongyang. They began to drill North Korean troops, many of whom were seasoned comrades of the Communist Chinese in their fight against the Nationalists in Manchuria. The Americans in the South, hell-bent on leaving, did not want Rhee to provoke North Korea. So they kept offensive weapons out of the hands of Republic of Korea troops, who were little more than a national police force. By July 1, 1949, U.S. combat troops were gone, leaving Rhee his paper army, five hundred American military advisers, and U.S. defensive military hardware. Six months later, having dropped all pretense that a divided Korea might be made whole, the United States rang down what it thought would be the final curtain of its brief Korean occupation when Secretary of State Dean Acheson declared the peninsula to be outside the American Far East defense perimeter.

North Korean leader Kim Il-sung knew a sitting duck when he saw one. Following consultations in Moscow, he placed his troops on ready alert along the 38th Parallel. At dawn on June 25, 1950, they swooped over the line, inundating the South's green, armorless army and quickly captured Seoul. Sniggering at a hasty United Nations resolution calling for a cessation of fighting, the North pressed its attack along both sides of the mountainous spine that bisects the peninsula, mincing all opposition.

That same UN resolution called on members to provide "such assistance as may be necessary" to the Republic of Korea in repelling the invaders, and, defense perimeter or no defense perimeter, the United States was the first to respond. The advance of Communist forces to within one hundred miles of the Strait of Korea, directly across from Japan, had prompted Acheson and President Truman to reassess Korea's strategic importance. Recalling the appeasement of Adolf Hitler as he methodically invaded his neighbors, they agreed that the Communists must be stopped in their tracks, even in so remote a place. From his base in Tokyo, U.S. Far East Commander Douglas MacArthur ordered the understaffed and undertrained Twenty-fourth Infantry Division, which had been engaged in routine occupational duties in Japan, into combat in Korea. No sooner had the first battalion—"Task Force Smith"—taken up positions near Osan than it was set upon by the North Koreans. After holding out for seven hours against incessant attack, and finding itself nearly surrounded, it broke out and fought its way south. The delay bought the Twenty-fourth's commander, flamboyant, bazooka-toting Maj. Gen. William F. Dean, time enough to deploy near Taejon, and for two weeks the Americans held the North Koreans at bay. General Dean, who was the last to leave Taejon, was captured. But his heroic stand gave the Twenty-fifth Division and the rest of the Eighth Army time to arrive and prepare a counterattack.

By early August the entire peninsula had been sealed by a UN naval blockade, and the combined Far East air forces had flown more than ten thousand bombing missions in support of American and South Korean troops and their UN allies. These sorties became the first blow to North Korea's lengthening supply lines. By late August better-equipped reinforcements had arrived from the American mainland, Okinawa, and Hawaii, and Lieut. Gen. Walton H. Walker was able to hold the Communist advance at bay at the Naktong River north and west of Pusan. UN troops would not be driven into the sea.

Rather than butt heads with the jubilant North Koreans at this Pusan Perimeter, MacArthur ordered a risky amphibious landing into the belly of the Communist beast. At dawn September 15, U.S. Marines landed on Wolmi Island in Inchon Harbor, hard by the 38th Parallel. Eleven days later they recaptured Seoul, and on that very day a U.S. armor division that had broken through the Pusan Perimeter linked up with the Seventh Division near Osan. The North Korean offensive had not just been broken, it had been been shattered. Demoralized Communist units used the cover of Korea's rugged mountains to escape back to the North, leaving behind more than 100,000 prisoners of this undeclared war.

Opposite. Units of the Marine First Cavalry Division, hastily brought up from Okinawa, prepare to disembark from an "LST" (Landing Ship/Tank) in the port of Pohang near the Pusan Perimeter on July 18, 1950. Though these ships were as large as a small tanker, they could edge as close as eight feet to shore to off-load troops, tanks, and other vehicles.

UN forces followed the U.S. Joint Chiefs of Staff's directive to "destroy the North Korean armed forces." They swept forward, pausing briefly at the 38th Parallel while General MacArthur got clearance to proceed into North Korean territory. On October 20, Pyongyang was captured by infantry and airborne units. The advance by Republic of Korea troops up North Korea's east coast was so unfettered that the port of Wonson fell before the U.S. X Corps could arrive to solidify the victory. The combined armies' onslaught, and the arrival of ROK Forces at the Yalu River on the Manchurian border at Chosan, placed the Chinese Communists on agitated alert. They could see without being told that it was MacArthur's plan to eliminate the North Korean army—and communism in Korea—for all time.

The Chinese had already supported the ragged remnants of North Korea's forces, but the scope of their massive build-up in Manchuria had been obscured by camouflage, the darkness of night, and the unwillingness of UN political leaders to authorize reconnoitering flights over Chinese territory. UN forces that were pressing toward the Manchurian and Soviet borders faced the same danger of overextended supply lines and surprise attack that the North Koreans had encountered outside Pusan. But MacArthur told Washington the Chinese would not dare risk world war by intervening in strength in Korea. The night of November 25–26, 1950, they proved him wrong, slamming into UN positions west of the mountains and the X Corps to the east with unfathomable thousands of troops. Their lightly equipped soldiers, slipping in and out of the forests, easily outflanked and then overwhelmed UN positions. In a flash, MacArthur's agenda turned from an advance to the Yalu to saving the entire UN command. He was prohibited from unleashing air assaults on Chinese bases in what he called their "privileged sanctuaries" in Manchuria. Truman did not want to risk widening the war, even though the Chinese had widened it for him. So MacArthur ordered a withdrawal. More than 100,000 UN forces on the east coast staggered south to the ports of Wonsan and Hungnam, with horrific loss of life and materiel. Their rescue by the U.S. Navy ranks among the most massive, best-executed evacuations in military history.

Above. *Marine Maj. Charles L. Schroeder of Long Island, New York, returns from another mission. Marine fighters provided close ground support to UN forces and helped choke off the flow of Communist supplies and reinforcements. But the enemy's mass movements usually occurred at night when they could not be spotted from the air.*

Opposite. *Pilots of the First Marine Aircraft wing aboard a carrier off Korea warm up their Corsair fighter-bombers preparatory to flight.*

Above. *GIs fought house to house when UN armies took the North Korean capital of Pyongyang in the massive push north of the 38th Parallel in October 1950. This rail station had already seen better days. Before the year was out, UN forces were forced back out of the city following the intervention of Chinese legions.*

Left. *A Marine rocket team fires a rain of death on retreating Chinese. These weapons threw out multiple rounds at once in a demoralizing ripple, but their consumption of ammo was voracious. The Marines had evacuated at Hungnam, swung down the coast to the Pusan area, and fought their way back north against the Chinese Communists.*

Opposite. *A Chinese soldier is questioned at the First Marine Division's Seventh Regimental command post near the Chosin Reservoir, within seventy-five miles of the Manchurian border, about two weeks before the massive Chinese invasion of Korea.*

Above. *Marine Tech. Sgt. John E. Boitnott of Comfort, North Carolina, left, and Pfc. Henry A. Riday of Nekoosa, Wisconsin, share a smoke. Foxholes and trenches appeared once battle lines stabilized along a jagged line that became the postwar "DMZ."*

Opposite. *Marine rocketeers let loose a spectacular and deadly fusillade during a night mission. Because of their inferiority in firepower, the Chinese, in particular, were deadly night fighters.*

General Walker was killed in a Jeep accident two days before Christmas, and command of all ground forces fell to Lieut. Gen. Matthew B. Ridgway, who consolidated forces at the 38th Parallel while pulling the remnants of X Corps back to Pusan to form a strategic reserve. Revived by the turn in fortunes, the North Koreans quickly reconstituted an army and joined the Chinese in a second invasion of South Korea on New Year's Eve. Seoul fell again on January 4, 1951, spilling thousands of panic-stricken civilians (and Communist spies) into the laps of beleaguered UN soldiers, who themselves were more than a little spooked by the fanaticism of the Chinese legions. All the while, diplomatic chatter approached theatre of the absurd, with war still undeclared and Peking insisting it had no forces in Korea at all—never mind the tens of thousands of "volunteers" of Chinese origin who might be on the peninsula.

UN forces preferred a strategy of "rolling with the punches," standing up to the Chinese throngs, then falling back while another outfit took its turn holding a position. But Ridgway wanted to test the true mettle of the Chinese. He ordered a regimental combat team east of Seoul to fight without retreating. Its losses were staggering, but the lines held. The Chinese had punched themselves out, never to seize the widespread initiative again. Ridgway quickly followed up with a counteroffensive, designed not just to reclaim territory, but also to begin obliterating enemy personnel and equipment. "Operation Ripper" proved so effective that Seoul was back in UN hands by mid-March. And UN troops pushed on, crossing the 38th again at great cost.

American GIs were in shock at the time, however, over word that MacArthur had been relieved of command by President Truman. Flouting a directive that he make no public statements without obtaining clearance, the old warrior had kept up the drumbeat for attacks on the Manchurian "sanctuary," had called for a blockade of Chinese ports, had popped open a diplomatic can of worms with his support for Nationalist Chinese leader Chiang Kai-shek on Formosa, and had asked for massive reinforcements from home. But Truman did not want to provoke the Soviet bear. Worried that all-out efforts in Korea would sap American strength in front of the Iron Curtain in Europe, he secretly committed to settling for a draw on the Korean Peninsula. When MacArthur brazenly demanded Chinese surrender, Truman sacked him.

The Communists launched yet another spring offensive, but this time could not sustain it, and UN forces counterpunched into the North once again along the east coast mountain depression called the "Punchbowl." To the west, troops under Eighth Army commander James A. Van Fleet captured Chorwon and Kumwah in the North, only to be stalled by the onset of monsoon rains. As trench warfare settled in, the Soviets' United Nations representative, Jakob Malik, proposed cease-fire negotiations, and truce talks were undertaken at Kaesong. As the Communists harped over such matters as the size of the peace table—and the thornier issue of whether Communist soldiers and North Korean civilians who had fled south could be forced to repatriate—the talks sputtered, then started again. But Van Fleet's troops were not waiting for a diplomatic settlement. They scored more small but significant victories and were poised for even more advances when Ridgway ordered him to cease offensive operations.

A wounded North Korean is administered first aid by Navy hospital corpsmen and Marine leathernecks. Enemy wounded were often surprised to receive humane treatment. Once UN casualties had been moved safely to M.A.S.H. units in the rear, seriously wounded enemy troops were also accommodated.

Above. *American soldiers round up captured North Korean troops. Unburdened by heavy boots, military hardware, or food rations (they carried rice in socks hung around their necks) these soldiers were highly mobile. Many wore tennis shoes, which aided both movement and stealth. Their winter garb, featuring lightweight quilted jackets, was only slightly more bulky.*

Left. *Seriously wounded North Korean soldiers lie where they fell. Navy hospital corpsmen accompanying the Marines later removed these men for medical attention and interrogation. Note the split trousers of the Korean at the left, which reveal white civilian clothes underneath. Communists played havoc by sneaking behind UN lines and attacking guerrilla fashion.*

By summer 1952, Gen. Mark W. Clark had replaced General Ridgway, who moved to Europe to command NATO forces, and the Korean War became a pivotal issue in the U.S. presidential campaign. When Gen. Dwight D. Eisenhower, the hero of D-Day, promised to end the war quickly if elected, then visited the front shortly after his landslide victory in November, the road to a settlement was oiled. As he later noted in his memoirs, absent satisfactory progress toward peace "we intended to move decisively without inhibition in our use of weapons, and would no longer be responsible for confining hostilities to the Korean Peninsula." In plain talk, Ike was brandishing nuclear weapons at China. By early June 1953, agreement seemed at hand, only to founder again over the repatriation issue. Rhee refused to be a party to any agreement that left the bisection of his country intact or that forced prisoners who did not want to to return to North Korea. General Clark bluntly informed Rhee that the alternative to his agreeing to an armistice would be the withdrawal of UN forces, throwing him to the Communist wolves, and the aging president finally assented to step back and keep quiet. On the July 27, 1953, the armistice was signed at Panmunjom, though not by the South Koreans. The conflict's final, zig-zagging battle line became a lasting demilitarized zone, the *de facto* border between North and South, and the repatriation of prisoners began. At last, Americans could resume their push for prosperity under the comforting hand of their genial president.

An estimated two million North Korean and Chinese soldiers had died in battle or of disease. UN losses are recounted for all time in inscriptions on the low ledge of the Korean War Veterans Memorial Pool of Remembrance:

Eight-inch guns of the U.S.S. Saint Paul fire at enemy gun positions in Hungnam Harbor the day before the final truce signing. The Navy's guns had been crucial in supporting the miraculous evacuation of UN forces facing the surprise Chinese onslaught in late 1950. But the Communists offered almost no naval target for these big guns.

Dead
USA	54,246
UN	628,833

Missing
USA	8,177
UN	470,267

Captured
USA	7,140
UN	92,970

Wounded
USA	103,284
UN	1,064,453

The terrible losses recall a thought from pioneer aviatrix Amelia Earhart, who wrote, "Courage is the price that life exacts for granting peace."

CHAPTER TWO

Service Beyond All Recompense

Every GI who set foot in Korea between 1950 and 1953 remembers the muck around denuded hillsides in the endless summer rain. The biting Siberian winds. The stench of human excrement, lovingly carried in buckets by Korean peasants to nurture rice shoots in the paddies; it was a stink so foul you could smell it offshore. The odor, too, of the dead, and the palpable scent of fear. The Korean War had no noble lulls in the fighting so each side could bury its dead under a flag of truce. Dead enemy soldiers lay where they fell until UN forces left the area. In the worst battles, piles of enemy dead were everywhere. When the battlefield was secure, grave-registration troops would remove UN casualties to the rear in mattress covers. Those who served in Korea saw and did things that they could share only with a buddy, or maybe a spouse, if they made it home. The worst experiences were best kept to themselves. Since there had been talk of an armistice for two years—and fits and starts toward one before it actually came—peace in Korea barely caused a stir back home. There were no wild V-K Day celebrations. For American combatants and support personnel, it was back to work, back to school, back to life, almost as if Korea had been a brief bad dream, best forgotten. Television, busy putting together its first cross-country networks, did not show their trials or triumphs. There were newspaper accounts, but no Ernie Pyle, no Mauldin cartoons. News of the war came from Washington, from Moscow, from Peking, and from the new UN as much as from press tents in Seoul. But the stories are coming out now, the feelings released, at a place of literal and figurative reflection: the Korean War Veterans Memorial. Just a few of these memories follow.

Harry Clark kept an extensive photo album of his days in Korea. One shows him hoisting a mortar shell that's half his size, and this candid view depicts one of the few treats on the front—a good wash with clean water.

Cleveland Moffett, Jr., was a clerk, working in a Washington, D.C., drug store when he was drafted in 1951. He served as an infantryman—an ammo carrier—in the First Cavalry, Fifth Regiment:

The first night I got there we pitched pup tents and slept near a college, a Korean college, right out of Inchon. Woke up the next morning in snow, I mean it's forty below zero, no lie. During the winter, thousands of guys got frostbitten. We went up to the front, and they put us in outfits. I went into heavy weapons, machine guns. After we got on the line, we dug in the bunkers, some of which were already there. We just cleaned them up. About two nights later the Chinese attacked, pushing civilians ahead of them with sticks so we couldn't fall on them. We had to fire to keep them off of us.

This bugle, they got this bugle. They blew it, and they tried to run us over, but they didn't make it on up. They kept coming in waves, plus they was doped up. Many peasants we shook down had opium, sacks of it, and we used to burn it. But when the summer come, and all these bodies thawed out, you couldn't believe the smell. We couldn't go in and clean 'em up 'cause of the mines, the barbed wire fences and all the stuff that we put in. So we had to live with the smell for awhile.

I'd been in the Naval Reserves before, but I wanted to be in the Army. I got a letter at my home in D.C., telling me to report to Bainbridge for Navy training. So I wrote back, "Sorry, I can't make it. In Korea on the front line."

Gaylin Poulson was a Redmond, Utah, high school student when the Korean War broke out. He joined the Air Force in 1952, qualified as an aircraft mechanic, and was assigned to flying weather reconnaissance missions over Formosa and Korea from Japan.

We looked down at the area of the 38th Parallel from ten thousand feet, and you could see all the pockmarks in the land from the bombs, and the craters where the shells had gone off. It had been a terrible, terrible conflict.

MacArthur was still over there, and he was a hero to the military because he was an aggressive soldier. He was there to win, and he would have won the war if President Truman would have allowed him to do it. When Truman fired MacArthur it was really a shock. Never in the history of the United States military had a general been so unceremoniously fired.

Of course, when he was relieved of his command, it was pretty obvious to us that winning the war wasn't the thing that we were over there to do. And that created a lot of concern in our minds: What were we doing there? And to this day they're still arguing over that 38th Parallel, North Korea and South Korea. They're still trying to reunite the two countries, and it doesn't look like it's going to happen for a long time yet.

Gaylin Poulson candidly admits that he and all his friends in Redmond, Utah, who enlisted joined the Air Force or Navy after three friends who'd been drafted into the Army were shot up in early Korean War fighting. Based in Japan, Poulson kept up with General MacArthur's high-profile career. He says MacArthur was a hero to both the Japanese and to American service personnel.

We came home, and we were all tickled to death because we had the GI Bill. We bought homes and settled down, but we never received any recognition, not that we were trying to receive any. We didn't even think about it until, later on, all these other causes started to be out on the forefront, seeking recognition. Then we wondered, why? Why didn't that happen to us, too?

Jack Murray got an early discharge from the Army in March 1950 because his dad had lost his job back in Abington, Massachusetts. His engineer battalion went on to Korea shortly after the war started. But when his father died in 1952, Murray re-enlisted and wound up as a staff sergeant in the engineer staff of I-Corps north of Seoul.

It was like the stalemates they talk about in World War I. The line was pretty stable, though there was a lot of activity, taking one hill, losing it, recapturing it. The Chinese were pushing, and we were trying to maintain our position the way it was. The armistice was coming up, and both sides were trying to get the best military position on these hills. I've since read that they lost more lives in this last year of the war than they did in the previous two, which surprised me in a way.

When I got home, the reaction was, "Murray, where you been? Ain't seen you around lately," things like that. No parades, but none of us expected any, because we were from the World War II era when our older brothers and uncles and so forth came home, and it was business as usual. The Fifties were the silent generation, you know. You didn't blow your own horn.

Al Ortiz was drafted out of high school in El Paso. Most of his fighting took place as a master sergeant with the Forty-fifth "Thunderbird Division," heading an infantry platoon on Hill 255 north of Seoul, which became known as "Pork Chop Hill" because of its shape as seen from the air.

We went, we saw, we met the enemy, we didn't conquer, we came home. For a year, I never had a chance to see anything but the front lines. The Chinese have been referred to as "hordes," and that's the way it was. Not to take away from the high rate of casualties that the ROK troops suffered when they were overrun, but you couldn't help but noticing there weren't a lot of [South] Koreans on the front. When I asked, I was told they were "being trained," but it did bother us that we were there doing their fighting.

There was never, ever enough ammunition, which always resulted in hand-to-hand combat. The Chinese would do everything they could to exhaust our ammunition. They would send men charging up a hill without anything, without any weapons whatsoever. The sole purpose was to get us to exhaust our ammunition. The second wave would come along, they had some weapons. Then the last batch would always make it to the top.

M. Sgt. Al Ortiz cut a dashing figure in Company E, 179th Infantry Regiment, of the Forty-fifth Division. But the uniform of the day was less stylish on the front lines, where he faced the oncoming Chinese waves.

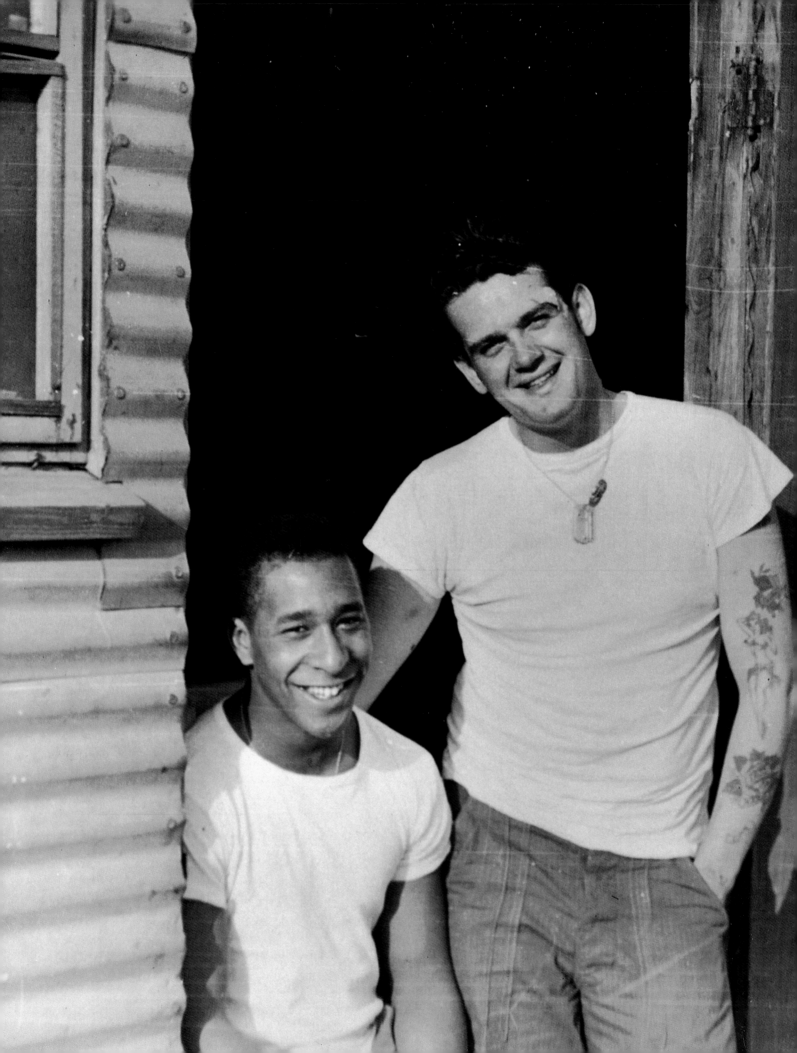

Dan Smith was finishing school in Winsted, Connecticut, when war broke out in Korea. He was drafted and ended up working as an operating room technician at the Eighth Army's 121st Evacuation Hospital in Korea.

The operating room job was a good job. We had milk, powdered eggs, sheets on our beds. But the work was haunting, prepping the serious cases. There was a sergeant who had just come back from the States, doing his last stint in Korea. He was on patrol duty on the front lines. He was coming back—no wounds, nothing—and his Jeep hit a mine. When he came in he was sitting on a stretcher. His arms were dangling. His legs were dangling. His face was all blasted away. We worked on him for about ten hours. We wheeled him in the recovery room, he was all bandaged up—couldn't see. I stopped by to see how he was doing. He says, "I can't wait to get back to the States and see my little daughter run across the room and give her a big hug." But what he didn't know was that he had lost two eyes, two legs, and two arms. We have a lot of veterans like that, stuffed in VA hospitals, but that's real war.

I came back and got my 26/26—you get $26 a week for twenty-six weeks, a lot of money at that time. I was eligible for the GI Bill for school and housing. I was healthy. I went to school, got an education, and I just felt very fortunate. But I found it challenging, to say the least, to fight some of the civil-rights battles as a black that I thought were over, based on my generally good experiences in the military, which was integrated in Korea for the first time.

Harry Clark was a miner in Jenkinjones, West Virginia, a tiny coal-mining town that no longer exists. Six months after the start of the Korean War, Clark enlisted and ended up as a Pfc. medical aide, and later a heavy mortarman with the Third Infantry Division.

It was so damn cold in the winter of '51–'52. I'd reach up and break the ice out of my moustache. Once it reached fifty-six below zero. Tanks rolled across rivers without falling through.

Ira Jett had graduated from high school in Fairfield, Illinois, in 1951 when he enlisted in the Army after the Navy and Air Force turned him down because he was married. He was a corporal in a military-intelligence unit at Fort Riley, Kansas, when he volunteered for Korean service.

I'd had ancestors in military service from the Revolutionary War on, so I figured, "It's my time to do my share." But I was shipped to Tokyo—never ended up in Korea itself until 1969. Over fifty percent of the men I served with were World War II soldiers, draftees. I think everyone had a patriotic sense that if the government needed them, if they had a war, we should do our share.

M. Sgt. Edward Caine, right, was Dan Smith's best friend back in Winsted, Connecticut. Caine, who was killed two days after writing home that all as "fairly quiet" in his sector, had shown his buddy the ropes and told him how to avoid front-line combat. Smith became a hospital emergency-room technician and saw the tragedy of wartime up close.

35

Joe Spilotro was working in a Chicago electronics plant when he was drafted. When he got to Inchon, an officer pointed to him and said, "We'll take you" as a medic.

The group I was with—the Fifth Regimental Combat Team—had captured about 400 Chinese prisoners. They had them all in a circle, with stones piled around, and barbed wire, and little cans with stones inside so they could be heard if they crawled out at night. They outnumbered us, you see, by about twenty-five to one. After about two weeks of training, they gave me a little kit bag and said, "OK, you go in there, and see if any of them are hurt, because they think we're trying to kill them." They had a lot of propaganda going around that told that we were terrible guys and would kill them. One of the interpreters taught me to say a Japanese word—not Chinese, Japanese—that means "hurt." A few of them understood this. Some of these people had shrapnel in their feet, because they wore tennis shoes.

I had trouble understanding what we were doing there, trying to fight a draw. I had heard that MacArthur got bounced because he wanted to use the atom bomb, and in my mind, that's the way war is fought. You try to win. It's hard to keep guys in a foxhole, risking their lives, and tell them, "All we want is a draw." Why pick me for this kind of work? Get somebody else.

Ray Donnelly, Jr. of Worcester, Massachusetts, was studying graphics in college when he joined the Army and was shipped to Korea, where he served as a master sergeant, a machine gunner in the Fifth Regimental Combat Team, a frontline portion of the Twentieth Division.

I admire everyone who knows exactly where they were over there, 'cause I didn't. I was on one hill, and every time they'd send us on patrol they'd give us a small map, and you just went to another hill. I mean, I had to wait for letters from home to find out where I was. After each attack, x amount would rotate, x amount would get hurt, x amount would get killed. They'd have to replace everybody. So you'd just get promoted, because you were there longer than anybody else. There was no great skill involved. You just kind of outlasted everybody else. Eighteen of us went over. I was the only one to come back alive.

You just developed your forty points. If you're on the front lines, you got four points a month. In the rear, you got three points a month. Way in the rear, you got two. Japan, you got one. Once you got forty points, you were on the rotation roster to go home. It would take them about a month to get you out of there. I had my forty points in the first ten months I was there.

The cold got to me. That's why I have crooked hands. They were frozen. I've had eleven operations. But my wife had it a lot worse than I did, because I knew when I was in trouble, and I knew when I could relax. She didn't. The World War II guys, they're the real heroes. I had a friend who spent five years in the jungles of New Guinea. My brothers-in-law had a ship shot out from under them. I spent one year. I wasn't about to go home and say, "Hey, look what I did." I got home on a Friday, went back to work Monday.

Good-natured Ray Donnelly saw nothing but tough fighting for ten straight months on the front in Korea. Of eighteen friends who went to the peninsula together, only he returned.

36

Regimental executive officer Sherman Pratt (standing, center) and other members of the Second Division await rotation out at Pusan after bloody fighting at Heartbreak Ridge in central Korea in late 1951.

Norb Reiner, of Johnstown, Pennsylvania, was attending Notre Dame University during the early months of the war. When Indiana was looking for replacement troops because it did not have enough on its draft register, Reiner enlisted and served in a special military intelligence unit north of Seoul.

It was a political war, very much of a political war: Don't do anything that will disrupt the talks at Panmunjom. But the war was worth the cost. History will justify this as the first stumbling block, the first impediment, the first serious resistance that the totalitarian world encountered—the first break in their dominance over people. I think they found out aggression is going to be difficult, no matter where we try it.

When I got home I caught up with my class in college. People didn't even know I'd been gone. I forgot the war myself until fifteen or sixteen years ago, when I got involved in some veterans' organizations.

Sherman Pratt, a World War II veteran, was on duty in his hometown of Little Rock, Arkansas, at the onset of hostilities in Korea. He was an infantry captain in Korea, where he joined the Twenty-third Regiment of the Second Division as a company commander just as they were breaking out of the Pusan Perimeter. He ended up in northwest Korea, well past the 38th Parallel.

When the Chinese intervened, the challenge was whether we could even save the Eighth Army. The strategy called for our division to stay behind and fight a rear-guard action, try to hold the Chinese off until they could get the bulk of the Eighth Army out. We got surrounded and cut off and had to fight our way back out. My division was slaughtered there. But we like to think that had we not stayed there and paid that price, that it may well be that the bulk of the Eighth Army would have been surrounded and cut off and perhaps annihilated. It was a terrible price to pay, but an unavoidable price, so the bulk of the Eighth Army could fight again another day.

We occupied the high ground in the middle of the night. I don't think the Chinese knew we were there. And by dawn the next morning they were climbing the hill by the hundreds and hundreds. We had a stiff firefight just at daybreak. We spent the whole day there—November the twenty-ninth, 1950—on the top of the hill, watching long lines of hundreds and thousands of Chinese marching around some five miles to our right and left. We were sitting there biting our fingernails, waiting and waiting for permission to withdraw. Permission finally came about four o'clock in the afternoon. The history books call it the Kunu-ri Withdrawal. But to us it's like saying "Gettysburg" or "Little Big Horn."

Cleveland Moffett returned to his clerk's job and remained in the Navy and Army reserves for thirty-two years. *Gaylin Poulson* and his wife own a printing and graphics business in suburban Denver. *Jack Murray* was a staff lawyer at the U.S. Congress for thirty years before establishing his own law practice. *Norb Reiner* became the director of operations for the national cemetery system of the Veterans Administration. *Dan Smith* retired from government service, designing health-education programs for the Department of Health and Human Resources. *Ray Donnelly* worked for the government in printing and graphics before retiring. *Joe Spilotro* retired from the Navy, where he had scheduled ship overhaul and maintenance. *Ira Jett* stayed in the military for twenty-two years, then worked for the federal Office of Personnel Management. *Al Ortiz* worked for the Foreign Service at two government agencies and developed educational programs for Hispanics at the new Washington Technical Institute in the Nation's Capital. *Sherman Pratt* completed a military career as a Pentagon military liaison to Congress, then worked as a Federal Communications Commission attorney. All but two of these men served as volunteers at the offices of the Korean War Veterans Memorial Advisory Board as it prepared for the July 1995 dedication of the memorial.

In its time, the settlement that ended the Korean War was called "peace without honor." The men and women who served there were told that they did not win.

But they did win their war. They confronted an invader and drove him out of a fledgling nation. They did all that they were allowed to do. Was it worth what for many was the ultimate price? Ask the forty million free Koreans in the world's eleventh-largest industrial nation.

Captain Pratt takes a break in a foxhole north of Wonju in central Korea. Twice promoted for his valorous combat record, he would continue in the service and became a noted military-affairs author and editor as well.

CHAPTER THREE

The Secretary of the Army

Has Asked Me to Express His Deep Regret

Back in Japan after his ordeal, Lieutenant Jones and his pregnant wife, Jerene, are reunited. Jones lost twenty-five pounds off his 165-pound frame as a result of the forced march and meager food during his captivity.

O*n September 3, 1950, Thomas Jones, a first lieutenant in Company D, Eighth Engineers of the First Cavalry Division, commanded a platoon of eight men as they worked their way down a steep trail along a three-thousand-foot mountain, under heavy enemy fire. The Koreans called the place "Sacred Mountain." Atop it loomed the old walled city of Ka-san and the Buddhist Poguk Temple. The GIs, though, gave it a more prosaic name: "Hill 902." By the time dawn broke on September 4, Jones knew that he and his men were in deep trouble. Two platoons to his left had been wiped out, and his own was now firmly in enemy territory. A mortar shell had wounded two of his men during the night, and over the next four days it became clear that no UN counterattack to retake the hill was possible. The men could not move by night because of fog and the treacherously steep terrain, or by day because of their exposed position. They were soon out of rations, soaked to the skin by rain, and wondering aloud if they would ever get off Hill 902.*

What happened next became a story of courage and perseverance of a kind that was not uncommon among those who served in Korea. It was a story that Jones, a bridge builder's son and West Point graduate from the farm town of Cerro Gordo, Illinois, himself would call "Two Hundred Miles to Freedom" in an account he wrote in a military engineering journal a year later. Excerpts reveal captivity's toll.

Suddenly I was awakened by voices shouting and yelling in Korean, to see the area swarming with Koreans. I hoped desperately that they were South Koreans, but as they drew near, I saw the red star in the center of their caps. My only reaction was to stand and wait. With our rusted weapons and only about four grenades, any resistance would have been hopeless.

A North Korean corporal had evidently been taking about fifty men to the top of the mountain when they accidently stumbled upon us. They appeared to be much more surprised than we were, probably because we were so far behind enemy lines. They took away our weapons and our watches, rings, wallets, and maps. We then started toward the top of the very mountain we had spent seven long, weary days descending.

Upon reaching the ridge line again, the Koreans took our dog tags and steel helmets, which heretofore we had been allowed to keep. As we stood there wondering what would happen next, an officer pulled out a pistol and placed it against the throat of one of our men. What we had all secretly feared while walking up the mountain was actually about to happen. The pictures of the murdered Americans on Hill 303 near Waegwan in the first day of the war flashed before my eyes. Hunger and fatigue had dulled our senses to such a degree that we had no strength to resist. Frantic, jumbled thoughts raced through my brain as I faced with the others what seemed to be the end. The officer slowly lowered the pistol, returned it to his holster, and began to laugh. His sense of humor almost killed us.

Before starting down the mountain, we were each handed a large ball of steaming rice. We ate all that our shrunken stomachs could hold and stuffed the rest into our pockets. We had gone only a few hundred feet when our guards forced us to exchange our combat boots for their rubber tennis shoes. In return for size 10½ C, I received a size 6, which necessitated cutting out the backs of the shoes and letting my heels overlap about three inches.

The men were fed rice and vegetable broth seasoned with cow entrails, and then marched for hours until their feet bled and blistered in their ill-fitting shoes. They were asked few military questions. Their captors seemed more interested in their families, jobs, and hopes once the war ended.

We reached the main road, and our two-hundred-mile trek to the 38th Parallel now started in earnest. Whenever our planes came over in the daytime, the Koreans took cover, or, if caught in the open, merely squatted down and ducked their heads. For about the first seventy-five miles we had two guards who were very friendly. We walked at our own pace, rested when we wanted to, and were allowed to rummage through deserted farmhouses for shoes, rags, food, and utensils.

Probably we could have escaped at any time while the first two guards were with us, but many factors prevented such an attempt. First of all, the bottoms of our feet were raw and covered with blood blisters, and our heels were painfully stone-bruised. Secondly, no gardens were visible in the immediate vicinity—just rice paddies and barren, shell-torn orchards. We needed a lot more food to regain our strength. The two wounded men were having trouble also, and we could not be sure how far they would be able to travel.

Left. *Thomas Jones finished second in his class at Cerro Gordo, Illinois, High School, where he was a football and basketball star and president of his senior class. After washing dishes at a sorority house to put himself through the University of Illinois, he joined the Army Air Corps with the intention of serving in World War II, but ended up at West Point instead.*

Opposite. *Company Commander Jones, at the Camp Zama staging area near Yokohama, Japan, would see his Eighth Engineer support battalion called up quickly for service in Korea in September 1950. The engineers, whose principal job was to build and maintain roads and bridges and set mines, were often called on as infantrymen as well.*

HEADQUARTERS, 8TH ENGINEER COMBAT BATTALION
OFFICE OF THE CHAPLAIN
APO 201, c/o POSTMASTER
SAN FRANCISCO,   CALIFORNIA

6 October 1950

Dear Jerry:

Colonel Holley is writing your Dad regarding Tom and it seemed only right that I should write you. I know how extremely anxious you must be regarding him.

As Colonel Holley has stated in his letter, soon after we had taken the Wall City I took a large party of men with me and we went into the Wall City, covering the ground there and the ground Dog Company covered in its ascent and withdrawal action. We did this in order to try and find the men from Dog Company who were missing as a result of this engagement. Every man in the party searched diligently but no trace could be found of either Tom or the other men of Dog Company.

You don't know how much I wish I could write you some word that would bolster your hope for in a sense I consider you and Tom my particular couple in the 8th Engineers. It was just about one year ago we had our conference regarding your marriage. I remember how at that time I felt you two would make a splendid couple. Since then I have had no reason to doubt my judgement.

Tom was a good officer and admired and respected not only by the officers of the Battalion but by all the men he had under his command. Everyone of them spoke highly of him. I am sure this must be a source of comfort and consolation to you during this time of sorrow and distress.

I have prayed that God would give you his help during these terrible anxious days. You may be sure my prayers will continue to be with you. I do know this, that your faith in God, the help he can give you and his Presence with you will give you the ability to carry on successfully and to make you the best kind of a mother for the child that will be yours before long.

God bless you Jerry, and may he give you of his strength and help.

Most Sincerely,

James H Goewey

JAMES H. GOEWEY
Chaplain (Capt) USA
Battalion Chaplain

They reached a schoolhouse, where Jones and his infantry sergeant were questioned for two days by a North Korean major who spoke excellent English.

The first hint of our ultimate destination now came out. The major told us, "When you get to Seoul [then in North Korean control], you will go to school every day and learn the true religion and what true democracy is. When our jets strafed the area, the major was terrified. We were forbidden to talk during any attack, but we did not find out until later that the North Koreans thought our pilots could hear them talking on the ground, and thus locate their positions.

The interrogation continued over many days, as the major tried to elicit information about American equipment and deployment.

Then came the prize question of all. "We think that since you are an officer you hear many rumors. What is MacArthur going to do after we capture Pusan? Do you think he will land more troops after we defeat the present army?" After another exasperating hour of explanation, the major was finally convinced that General MacArthur had not taken me into his confidence before I left Japan.

*About this time, Jones's mother, Jean, received a dreaded telegram at her home in Connecticut. It read, "*THE SECRETARY OF THE ARMY HAS ASKED ME TO EXPRESS HIS DEEP REGRET THAT YOUR SON IST LT. JONES THOMAS T. HAS BEEN MISSING IN ACTION IN KOREA SINCE 4 SEPTEMBER 1950.*" Jones's wife Jerene, whom the young lieutenant had met and married in Japan seven months earlier, was still in Tokyo. She was pregnant when her telegram arrived.*

The sergeant and I returned to the schoolhouse to discover that only one guard was left and the other prisoners had gone. We headed north with our guard. About five o'clock we arrived at Uisong and were led into a filthy cramped shack where we found about twenty South Korean prisoners. From this day on, our treatment took a radical change for the worse.

The guard allowed us to leave the dark shack only to eat or go to the toilet. The toilet consisted of an arbitrary line about ten yards from the shack and was used by about forty men. Each day we were given two meals consisting of two bowls of plain boiled wheat for which we waged a constant battle with a swarm of flies that deserted the latrine area at mealtime.

The men were lined up on a road and marched north again. Jones soon discovered he could endure the pounding to his emaciated body more comfortably by throwing away the size 6 tennis shoes and wrapping his feet in stolen cloth and cotton wadding. Once, they were strafed by a UN plane that disabled a locomotive in the middle of a bridge. While North Koreans frantically carried water to the stranded locomotive, the prisoners were forced to crawl past it on the damaged bridge. They arrived at another schoolhouse in Pungsan and were overjoyed to be joined by the prisoners from whom they had been separated. They were fed boiled oats with hot sauce, garlic, and rock salt flavoring.

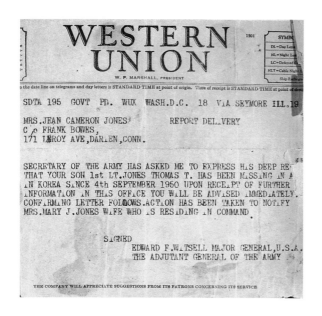

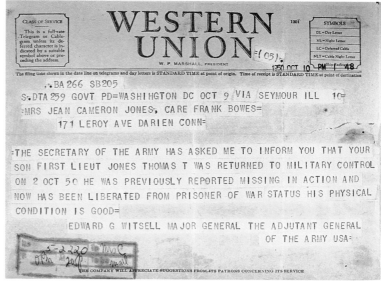

There was little to do during the six long days we remained here. A daily ritual, as soon as the sun had warmed up the room, was to de-louse ourselves. We used the simple and primitive method of removing one garment at a time and diligently searching for the lice. Fortunately I was allowed to keep my glasses. The next day we saw several of the Koreans using pages of the Bible for cigarette paper. We began to ask them for cigarette paper and, thus, recovered a few pages of the Bible.

The men marched on, wracked by dysentery, fatigue, and weakness from a shortage of vitamins. One man's lung ruptured, and he was in excruciating pain. The Americans' guards allowed them to construct a heavy wooden stretcher for him, which they took turns carrying on their shoulders, one hundred yards at a time. Finally, at an aid station, the sick and wounded were left behind. About dusk on October 1, as the fourteen remaining American prisoners were eating steamed rice, there was a loud commotion. The guards ordered Jones and his men to their feet and back onto the road, which was clogged with civilians, trucks, carts, and soldiers, all rushing to the north. In the confusion Jones, another lieutenant, and two Pfc.s fell behind and blended in among civilians at the side of the road.

While the endless procession of troops passed by, we bent over, pretending to fix our shoes to hide our bearded faces. When a break finally came in the column on the road, we managed to slip into the concealment of a thick hedge.

The men ran to a deserted farmhouse, where they found a sack of garlic, a box of seeds, and some straw mats. They hid through the night, then grubbed out some radishes and onions from a garden, and plucked a pumpkin off its vine. The food made a veritable banquet.

Some rounds of artillery fire landed about three hundred yards to our rear, having come from the direction of Chunchon. We then knew that our troops were in possession of the town, but we did not know who was between us and our own lines.

Kaesong, Korea
12 Oct 50

Dear Lt Jones—

The news of your restoring yourself to duty via the heel and toe
hit us yesterday through the Stars and Stripes of the 7th. I can't
begin to tell you how glad we all were to learn of your escape. There
was not a man in Company "C" who did not break out with a million dollar
smile when the news arrived. Frankly Sir, we had all just about given
you up as we had eye-witness, I was there accounts of how you were
1. Seriously wounded and unable to move; 2. Captured; 3. Dead in
a rice paddy. At the time you were reported missing we organized a
squad of volunteers to go in after you but could not get permission.

Things have been just about the same in the Company since you left—
a few new faces, Lt Whelan gone, Lt Skanse with the 3rd Platoon and
Sgt Pratt who is now acting Platoon Leader 1st Platoon. City Hall
pressure remains about the same except we have been moving to fast
for all of it to keep up with us.

Again, the news we received relative to you was about the best
smell we have encountered since we landed here. All the Platoon Sgts
send their best and we all hope to see you soon, In Japan I mean.

Your 1st Sgt

Robert H. Coughors.

They had seen civilians prowling around the house and decided to grab one in hopes of finding a way to freedom. A man came
to the door and turned the handle as the Americans clutched make-
shift knives.

The Korean started to come in; then he saw us, and
without a word closed the door and started away. We
stopped him, and in Korean we said, "Chingo, Chingo,"
meaning "friend." He shook our hands and grinned. Then
he gathered four of his friends, and we were taken to a house
partly concealed in a wooded gully.

*Not just Lieutenant Jones's
family was thrilled to have him
home. So were his men.*

Once inside, they brought out the UN flag and the South Korean flag and told us that they were a democratic people's band. By use of a crude map, they explained that the UN troops had landed at Inchon, had broken out of the Pusan Perimeter, and that our own forces were in possession of Chunchon!

Jones wrote a note, addressed to "An American Officer," explaining their situation and including obscure stateside facts, so the officer would know there was no trap. After four hours, the messenger returned with instructions to follow him.

When we got outside, we were taken right down the middle of the road, with the Koreans waving South Korean flags. We felt terribly uneasy, but we had little choice except to trust and follow them. Then, down the road, we saw what evidently was a South Korean patrol waiting for us about two hundred yards away with a Jeep. We continued walking and had gone about fifty yards when the Koreans took hold of our hands and started to run. When we were about seventy-five yards from the patrol, we were suddenly shot at from the rear. The patrol up ahead hit the dirt and returned fire over our heads.

Several bullets zinged over our heads and convinced us that someone was after us. Then we reached an open expanse of dry rice paddies and began crawling through them on all fours. Upon reaching the road we were met by a South Korean major in a Jeep. When he asked if I were Lieutenant Jones, I knew he had received the note. After a fast trip, we reached the regimental headquarters of the Second Regiment, Sixth ROK Division in Chunchon. Once inside the building, we burst into tears. It took us several hours to realize that after twenty-one days as prisoners, we had completed our two-hundred-mile walk to Freedom!

Jones's mother soon received a second telegram from the Adjutant General of the Army, informing her that her son had been liberated and that his physical condition was good. Thomas Jones got an engineering master's degree but stayed in the Army as a battalion commander, staff member of the Joint Chiefs at the Pentagon, and instructor at West Point before retiring from the service as a colonel in 1970. He then began a second career at the Federal Reserve Board as a management analyst, before retiring for good in 1984.

Thomas Tytherleigh Jones died from complications of Alzheimer's disease in 1994. In a eulogy, his son, Andrew, wrote, "He taught me about sacrifice through his duty to his family and his country. From him, I learned about courage and bravery, that it was okay to be afraid; that mastering fear and willing oneself to action is the hallmark of a truly brave man. This I know, because my father was such a man."

Opposite "Jerry" and Tom Jones share a laugh in this publicity photo, taken for the benefit of the many newspapers that wanted to tell the young lieutenant's story. The couple met at a dance in Japan, where Jerene's father was chief of staff for the Engineer Far East Command.

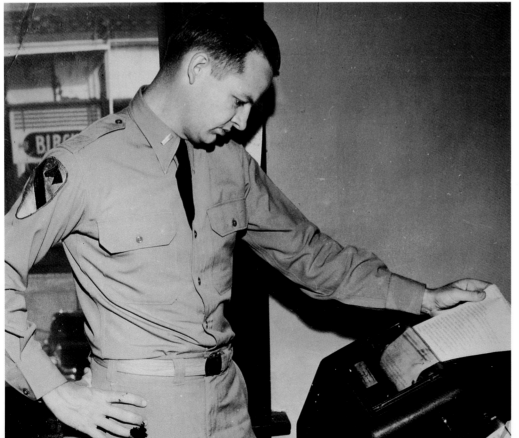

Left. *Lieutenant Jones checks a news wire account of his capture and escape. Desperately searching for information, Jones's family discovered there were 28 Thomas T. Joneses serving in the Korean theater of war. What eased the search slightly was that their Thomas T. Jones was the only officer—and for sure the only one with the middle name "Tytherleigh."*

CHAPTER FOUR

Honoring Those Who Fought

to Save Another's Freedom

Thirty-three years after the American men and women of the Korean War came home, Congress at last recognized their sacrifice and record of selfless service by authorizing a new Korean War Veterans Memorial. Not a war memorial, a veterans' memorial, to at long last thank not just those who fell, but all those who went to an unfamiliar land to defend another nation's freedom, and, therefore, our own.

Because of the welter of agencies involved in making a memorial on the Washington Mall a reality, it took three times longer to approve, design, and build the Korean War Veterans Memorial than it took to fight the war. The finished memorial, placed in a wooded grove on the Mall that had once been a nineteenth-century Army Corps of Engineers landfill, cost just over $18 million. The bulk of it was raised from small donations by veterans, the sale of a congressionally authorized one-dollar commemorative coin, and corporate contributions, most notably from Hyundai Motor America, Samsung Information Systems and other Korean firms with operations in America.

Opposite. *The sun's angle, a blustery and cloudy day, and the time of day all dramatically change the perception of the memorial's artistic elements.*

Overleaf. *Be alert. You are entering open terrain.*

Above. *The squad leader shouts directions to his radio man.*

More than five hundred firms or individuals entered the memorial's design competition. The winning concept, by a team of Pennsylvania State University architects who call themselves BL3, struck a chord with the memorial's presidentially appointed board of directors, all volunteers and Korean War veterans. It was a column of battle-clad soldiers, resolutely moving up a hill toward an American flag, and perhaps metaphorically toward home. BL3 ultimately resigned when their abstract conceptualizations were put through the wringer of comments, committees, and changes needed to win approval. The Washington firm of Cooper•Lecky Architects, which had shepherded the successful-beyond-all-dreams Vietnam Veterans Memorial, was awarded the task of making the Korean War Veterans Memorial a reality in the role of architects and art coordinators.

It was soon decided that this memorial would honor, but not name, the Korean War dead. It was not to be another eternal gravestone. It must commemorate all who served, not just those who carried carbines. It must reflect the contributions and sacrifices of the twenty-two other UN nations that fought alongside Americans.

Opposite. *The thousands of faces of support forces look out on the patrol.*

54

Opposite. *The lofty American flag, symbol of this free nation, stands at the apex of the Korean War Veterans Memorial, unifying the triangular field of service and the circular Pool of Remembrance.*

Above. *The squad leader barks directions to the troops.*

Opposite. *Always on the*
alert for hostile activity, an
Army rifleman moves warily
with his comrades.

Cooper•Lecky retained author and historian John Beardsley to help find a suitable sculptor for the memorial. Frank
C. Gaylord II of Barre, Vermont, a World War II combat veteran who made a riveting oral presentation on behalf of his
three-dimensional studies of the trooper statues, was selected
as the memorial's sculptor. His assignment: create a battle-
ready combat patrol in which each figure was assigned a
specific branch of service, rank, ethnicity, and military func-
tion. The original concept called for thirty-eight troopers,
symbolizing the 38th Parallel and the thirty-eight-month du-
ration of the war. But the number proved too large for the al-
lotted space and put the soldiers much too close together to
accurately represent troops on patrol. The memorial's second
element, a polished granite wall, helped to solve the numbers
problem: The nineteen figures would each be reflected in the
wall to achieve the symbolic thirty-eight number.

Above. *Etched faces in*
the granite, and stainless
steel ground troops, catch
the morning sun.

Opposite. *The Lincoln Memorial provides a fitting backdrop to its new neighbor on the Washington Mall.*

Above. *Army boots slog through the uneven terrain of the memorial.*

61

Left. *The machine gunner makes contact with his ammunition bearer.*

Opposite. *Support personnel appear in constellations on the wall. This is the artillery constellation.*

After extended debate with Cooper and Lecky, the sculptor and the Advisory Board agreed to clad the troopers in wind-blown ponchos, which conjure up northern Korea's nightmarish weather, blur specific insignias, and help downplay the soldiers' military hardware. Likewise, after six-, seven-, and eight-foot-tall figures were tested, seven was chosen. The figures appear slightly larger than life, but not menacing. The foot soldiers are shown advancing warily out of the woods, "chattering" among themselves by voice and gesture. Gaylord worked in unpolished stainless steel in order to give the figures detail, definition and a raw, virile quality reminiscent of the black-and-white photos of the conflict.

At one period during the Korean War, more than 300,000 UN forces were at work in the field and behind the scenes. How to honor the support personnel? Cooper, Lecky, and Beardsley selected muralist Louis Nelson of New York City to develop a mural to be etched into a polished granite wall, which flanks the columns of the troopers. The wall is 164 feet long and ranging in height from eleven to 4½ feet as the terrain rises. It incorporated more than twenty-four thousand faces computer-copied from anonymous photographs at the National Archives. Nelson likes to refer to this wall as "the nation's mantelpiece," reminiscent of a proud display of the photos of sons and daughters away at war. The first step in the design process was to generate a "constellation map" whose groups of "stars" were later exchanged for the faces of chaplains and mechanics and nurses and MPs and thousands of other military team members. After many trials, the precise texture of incision was achieved in the polished granite to create each delicate image.

Top left. *Distinctive headgear often identifies the role each support-team member plays.*

Bottom left. *The thousands of faces of support forces look out on the patrol.*

Top right. *Dedicated nurses often spelled the difference between life and death for Americans in the field in Korea.*

Bottom right. *M.A.S.H. units worked long and hard just behind the front lines in Korea. The television show accentuated the lighter moments between inbound evacuation flights. Then the personnel was "all business."*

Top left. *The Navy was at the ready in Korea, imposing an impregnable blockade, bombing port cities, and supporting evacuations where needed.*

Bottom left. *Visitors report seeing loved ones or old buddies—or even themselves— in the memorial's wall, even when the image is probably someone else, unknown. Either way, memories pour forth.*

Top right. *The faces of the memorial wall become part of the surrounding landscape.*

Bottom right. *Naval forces show the grim determination of all who served in the Korean conflict.*

Above. *Tense and alert,*
a soldier turns to check his
rear flank.

Opposite. *An Army trooper*
checks his right flank while
keeping in step.

Opposite. *An Army artillery field observer scans the horizon.*

Because of the multiple messages already inherent in the design, Cooper•Lecky and the Advisory Board were reluctant to clutter the memorial with allegorical inscriptions. Because of the memorial's prominent location on the national Mall, Kent Cooper had long been concerned that it give voice to the general theme of military service to country, as well as honoring those who served and fell in Korea. Cooper led the effort to develop two brief but powerful messages.

When Secretary of Defense Frank Carlucci marked the thirty-fifth anniversary of the cease-fire ending the Korean War, he spoke of the willingness of America's uniformed sons and daughters who took up arms to defend a distant nation. His words where adapted for the dedicatory statement for the memorial's Field of Service:

OUR NATION HONORS
HER UNIFORMED SONS AND DAUGHTERS
WHO ANSWERED THEIR COUNTRY'S CALL
TO DEFEND A COUNTRY THEY DID NOT KNOW
AND A PEOPLE THEY HAD NEVER MET

Above. *Bands of polished granite suggest the tilled terrain in parts of Korea. The incline leading toward the American flag is far gentler than the rugged climb of a Korean mountainside, necessitated to be sure the memorial is fully accessible to the physically challenged.*

Overleaf. *Two columns of ground troops move through the "Field of Service" toward the flag. The rear guard, just out of the woods, cautions the visitor to proceed attentively and with caution.*

69

Above. *Troops move together but at a healthy distance from one another, so that a grenade or mortar round would not take out the whole unit.*

Opposite. *The column moves forward with pride and purpose.*

The words were inlaid into an eight-ton triangular stone beneath the great flagpole—turning the visitor's eye back into the field of troopers and the wall of faces.

An even bolder, more profound, and simpler statement was chosen as the second focal point where the mural wall penetrates the water of a circular reflecting pool that is a place for *reflection* on the dead, wounded, captured, and missing of the war. The powerful saying was borrowed from the memorial's own Advisory Board, which saw it above the entrance to the American Legion headquarters building in Washington (no one there is completely sure where it originated). It consists of a reminder:

FREEDOM IS NOT FREE

The unprecedented impact of the Vietnam Veterans Memorial directly across the Mall, which became the nation's most-visited monument, prompted many veterans to suggest a similar wall for names of the Korean War dead. After heated debate, the suggestion was rejected as being duplicative and neglectful of others who served. The solution is a National Park Service kiosk at the head of the walkway leading into the memorial, where interactive computer screens flash endless images of those who died in Korea, often in the prime of their youth. Visitors may punch up a known name and see the person's service record and other background, as well as snapshots and portraits where available from families or friends.

The memorial takes on radically different appearances in the sun, in shade, in rain and snow, and especially at night, when a remarkable fiber-optic lighting system casts soft, subtle light on the wall and stark, pinpoint beams on the faces of the soldiers.

Among the most powerful of experiences at the Korean War Veterans Memorial is the mingling of images in the memorial wall—not just of the thousands of faces etched there and the ghostly reflections of the field of troopers—but also one's own.

Speaking about the sculpture, William Lecky said, "There's no question that there was healthy conflict between what the client wanted, which was something very realistic and militarily accurate, and what the reviewing commissions—the artistic side, if you will—preferred, which was something more abstract. The final solution was what we like to call "impressionistic styling," which makes it very clear what is being portrayed, but diminishes the sense of an actual collection of ground troops moving across the Mall."

Above. *Each trooper carries a weapon as well as many pounds of gear.*

Opposite. *The Washington Monument punctuates the skyline in the distance.*

Top left. *A BAR gunner hears a sound in the brush.*

Bottom left. *The statues' ponchos remind visitors of Korea's harsh conditions and add continuity to the nineteen troopers.*

Top right. *A Marine stays ever alert and cautious when on the march.*

Bottom right. *An Air Force observer scans the sky for enemy aircraft.*

Opposite. *A Marine assistant gunner keeps up the pace.*

Above. *Vigilance was the watchword on patrol.*

Right. *The nineteen ground troopers are reflected amongst the haunting faces etched into the memorial's mural wall.*

CHAPTER FIVE

A Message for All

The Pool of Remembrance is a place for quiet reflection on the cost of serving the cause of freedom.

Even before the Korean War Veterans Memorial could be dedicated, when construction barriers and fences were still obscuring the site, vets of that war and their families found a way to see it. Robert Hansen, executive director of the memorial's Advisory Board, tells of a group of marines who had graduated from basic training together on June 6, 1950, just in time to be shipped together to Korea. "Obviously many didn't come home," he said. "Those who did and are still living came to see the memorial, and it was almost impossible to get them to leave. They were overwhelmed with memories, as if the images took them back to the battlefield."

Hansen calls the memorial a "magnificent work of art, but more than that, I venture to say no memorial in the country, if not the world, truly honors the veteran and his or her dedication to the cause of freedom the way this one does. And it does it in so many ways. I feel a veteran can visit this memorial ten times and see something different each time."

Others think they see themselves, a relative, or a friend etched in the wall of faces, even though a match is improbable at best. When the wall was being finished in Cold Spring, Minnesota, a worker set down his sandblasting tool and started to cry. Asked what was troubling him, he replied, "That's my father."

Rob Smedley was the project architect who oversaw the construction. "It's working exactly the way I think we had all imagined it," he said. "The Pool of Remembrance is a very quiet, contemplative space. You're in amongst the trees. You're looking at the major theme of this whole commemorative park—that freedom is not free—and every single person in that war had to sacrifice in some way for the cause of freedom."

Above. *Visitor paths converge at the Pool of Remembrance.*

Right. *At the apex, the column of troopers converges on the dedication stone at the foot of the flagpole.*

Overleaf. *A ring of pleached linden trees surrounds the contemplative Pool of Remembrance.*

FREEDOM IS NOT FREE

DEAD
U.S.A. 54,246 U.N. 628,833

Above. *Opposite the "*FREEDOM IS NOT FREE*" inscriptions are tallies of cost of this war to preserve that freedom.*

One veteran said he would be back during the first bitter-cold, snowy winter day. "That," he said, "was Korea." Another described his visit as "mystical—ghostly, almost." Another found himself staring at the faces. "I know him," he'd say, then move on to another figure. "He didn't come back." One vet said he thought the memorial would be invaluable for school groups, helping them lift the Korean War beyond "two paragraphs in a textbook" and bring children the sense of danger and dedication that a different generation faced in combat. Someone else remarked, "A lot is said about the Vietnam Memorial and how it has helped the nation heal wounds. Well, many Korean War vets have healing to do, too. This will help. This will let some of the feelings out— not just feelings of fear in combat long repressed, or resentment at a lack of recognition, but also great feelings of pride in what they'd done."

Several visitors approved of the memorial's placement in a triad with the Lincoln Memorial and the Vietnam Veterans Memorial. "War has heroes like Lincoln," one said. "War kills as the Vietnam Memorial reminds us, and war is a time of unsung service, which this memorial will bring home."

Opposite. *A ground trooper is reflected in the faces of the armored forces who support him.*

Opposite. *Lights from the Lincoln Memorial cast a glow on the new Korean War Veterans Memorial.*

Above. *Soft light catches the face of the lead scout at nightfall.*

Overleaf. *A sea of support forces looks out on the lead ground trooper.*

Above. *A tank corpsman stands at the ready.*

Perhaps no other American was as intertwined with the memorial's meaning and the work that made it a reality as Col. William E. Weber, USA (Ret). A Milwaukee native, veteran of the occupation of Japan at the end of World War II, he was a company commander at Fort Campbell, Kentucky, when the Korean War broke out. Soon, as he puts it, he was "jumping out of airplanes" into fierce firefights with the North Koreans. He speaks quietly of his airborne division's "decimating" this North Korean party or "chewing up" that Chinese army.

But it was he who was chewed up by a Chinese hand grenade as he and his men were struggling to take yet another hill. He lost a leg and part of his right arm, and gained a load of fragments that were still floating loose inside his skull. After Swedish army nurses saved him in Korea, and military doctors in Michigan helped him back to health, he talked his way back into active duty. He taught at army colleges, pulled Pentagon duty, and volunteered his time working with disabled military personnel and servicemen incarcerated in civilian jails. And in 1987, President Reagan named him to the Korean War Veterans Memorial Board.

"The memorial does not glorify war or deify an individual," he says. "It presents the strength that is inherent in the diversity of our people when we unite in a common goal. It's not a memorial of grief. It's a memorial of pride." The nation has always been shielded from the realities of war, he noted. "Gruesome photographs are censored; everybody dies a heroic death. Well they don't all die a heroic death, but their deaths can be worth something, as this memorial makes clear. I am overwhelmed, not with its magnitude, but with its magnificence."

Long after the remaining survivors, like their war, are forgotten, the Korean War Veterans Memorial will stand as a testimonial to men and women of all generations, all wars, all ranks, and all stations who answer the nation's call to duty.

Opposite. Andrew Jones sought out a combat engineers' grouping on the memorial wall and pauses to remember his late father, whose story of heroic escape from captivity in Korea is told in this volume. Andrew is wearing his father's graduation ring from West Point, also seen in the photo of Thomas Jones on page 49.

ACKNOWLEDGMENTS

The authors gratefully salute and acknowledge the invaluable assistance of Kent Cooper and William Lecky of Cooper•Lecky Architects; Rick Dean of the U.S. Army Corps of Engineers; Robert Hansen, executive director of the Korean War Veterans Memorial Advisory Board; board member Col. William E. Weber, USA (Ret); the many tireless volunteers in the board's offices; and the curators at the National Archives in Washington, D.C., and the U.S. Army Military History Institute in Carlisle, Pennsylvania. We also extend our appreciation to Dino D'Angelo of Carol M. Highsmith Photography for his superb and untiring contributions to the photographs in this volume, and to Rob Smedley, Lance Davis, Melanie Hartwig-Davis, Mark Hutto, Gary Bouthillette, Karen Murray, and Louise Cook at Cooper•Lecky for facilitating our work at the memorial site.

Opposite. *A ghostly trooper from the Field of Service joins support units on the memorial's polished wall.*

Back endleaf. *An architectural rendering of the memorial by Paul Stevenson Oles begins to hint at the reflections that would highlight the visitor experience. At the time he completed this sketch, the memorial was in pieces far from the final site. Oles used detailed photographs of the sculptor's study models to envision the final interaction of figures and wall.*

KOREAN WAR VETERANS MEMORIAL
IN THE NATION'S CAPITAL

Established by the
AMERICAN BATTLE MONUMENTS COMMISION
and the
KOREAN WAR VETERANS MEMORIAL ADVISORY BOARD

Architects
COOPER•LECKY ARCHITECTS

Sculptor
FRANK C. GAYLORD, II

Muralist
LOUIS NELSON ASSOCIATES

Building and Fabrication
FAITH CONSTRUCTION, INC.
R. J. CROWLEY, INC.
COLD SPRING GRANITE COMPANY
TALLIX ART FOUNDRY

Engineering and Consulting
JOHN BEARDSLEY ~ ART CONSULTANT
WILES, DAILEY, PRONSKE ~ CIVIL ENGINEERING
ARNOLD ASSOCIATES ~ LANDSCAPE ARCHITECTURE
JAMES MADISON CUTTS ~ STRUCTURAL ENGINEERING
JOHN J. CHRISTIE & ASSOC. ~ STRUCTURAL ENGINEERING
SCHARF GODFREY ~ COST ESTIMATORS
CLAUDE R. ENGLE LIGHTING CONSULTANTS
WILLIAM HOBBS, LTD. ~ FOUNTAIN CONSULTANT
HOWARD•REVIS DESIGN ~ GRAPHIC CONSULTANT
BLAIR, DUBILIER & ASSOC. ~ VETERANS HONOR ROLL

Design and Construction Agent
U.S. ARMY CORPS OF ENGINEERS, BALTIMORE DISTRICT